HISTORY

Series Titles

THE INDUSTRIAL REVOLUTION
was created and produced by McRae Books Srl
Via del Salviatino, 1 — 50016 — Fiesole, Florence
(Italy)
info@mcraebooks.com
www.mcraebooks.com

Publishers: Anne McRae, Marco Nardi
Series Editor: Anne McRae
Author: Neil Morris
Main Illustrations: Lorenzo Cecchi pp. 18-19; Giacinto
Gaudenzi pp. 14–15, 36–37; MMcomunicazione (M.
Cappon, M. Favilli,G. Sbragi, C. Scutti) pp. 6-7,
16–17, 24–25, 34–35; Sergio pp. 8–9
Other Illustrations: Studio Stalio (Alessandro Cantucci,
Fabiano Fabbrucci, Margherita Salvadori)
Maps: Paola Baldanzi
Photography: Bridgeman Art Library, London: 10–11,
12–13, 20–21, 22–23, 26–27, 28–29, 32–33, 38–39,
40–41, 42–43, 44–45
Art Director: Marco Nardi
Layouts: Starry Dog Books Ltd
Project Editor: Loredana Agosta
Research: Loredana Agosta
Repro: Litocolor, Florence

Consultant: Pat Hudson is Professor of History at
Cardiff University. Her background and training are in
Economic and Social History. She is currently the
Book Review Editor of the Economic History Review.
She was President of the Economic History Society
2000-2004 and has been an Academician of the
Academy of the Social Sciences since its foundation
in 1999.

Library of Congress Cataloging-in-Publication Data

The Industrial Revolution
 ISBN 9788860981776

2009923559

Printed and bound in Malaysia.

HISTORY

The Industrial Revolution

Neil Morris

Consultant: Pat Hudson is Professor of History at Cardiff University. Her background and training are in Economic and Social History.

Zak
BOOKS

Contents

The Industrial Revolution changed the working habits of women. Many took factory jobs.

TIMELINE

	1700	1725	1750	1775
INDUSTRIAL INNOVATION	Abraham Darby smelts iron with coke instead of charcoal. Thomas Newcomen invents the steam engine.	John Kay invents the flying shuttle.	Selective breeding is used to produce New Leicester sheep.	Richard Arkwright opens a water-powered mill, helping to pioneer the factory system. The first steam-powered mills appear.
GREAT BRITAIN			Josiah Wedgwood opens a pottery-making factory in Staffordshire.	Matthew Boulton and James Watt open a steam-engine factory in Birmingham. The first iron bridge spans the Severn River in Shropshire.
BELGIUM AND FRANCE				
GERMANY			Ewald Georg von Kleist and Pieter van Musschenbroek (in Leiden) independently create a device that stores an electric charge.	
UNITED STATES OF AMERICA				
RUSSIA				
JAPAN				

Introduction

The Industrial Revolution brought about a long period of transition, during which a society dominated by agriculture changed into one characterized by increasing trade, industry, and finance. The invention of new machines drove this so-called revolution and led to the building of factories to house them. Working conditions in the factories were usually poor, and machine-minders worked long hours for little pay. Industrial towns sprang up, where housing was often overcrowded and unsanitary. Nevertheless, industrial growth brought the benefits of new, cheaper goods, as well as steam-powered methods of transportation. Eventually, social reformers succeeded in improving working conditions, housing, and education for working-class families. This book tells the story of the Industrial Revolution, from its beginnings in Britain, through its spread to other European countries, the United States, Russia, and Japan. The revolution took different forms around the world, depending on natural resources and politics, but its impact was enormous everywhere.

Scottish engineer James Watt (1736–1819), produced an improved steam engine that was used for many industrial purposes.

This American steam engine was made in 1869 to speed up and improve farming methods. It was used to drive mechanical threshers and sawmills.

1800	1825	1850	1875	1900

Steam locomotives are used for public railway.

English landowners are allowed to enclose land without referring to Parliament.

The Leeds–Liverpool Canal is completed.

The Great Exhibition opens in Hyde Park, London.

The coal mines of the Borinage region are updated with conveyor belts, leading to an increase in coal output.

The first Belgian railway links Brussels with Mechelen.

First public railway in France opens between Paris and Saint Germain.

Alfred Krupp introduces the open-hearth steel-making process in his factory in Essen.

Werner von Siemens builds the first electric railroad.

The New York Stock & Exchange Board is established.

The first US passenger train steams along a local line in South Carolina.

Charles Goodyear discovers vulcanization, a process of making rubber stronger.

Edwin Drake strikes oil near Titusville, Pennsylvania.

The first continuous railroad track across the US are completed.

Andrew Carnegie forms the Carnegie Steel Company.

The Trans-Siberian Railroad is begun.

Tsar Alexander II frees Russia's serfs.

The Nobel Oil Extracting Partnership is founded in Baku.

Commodore Perry's squadron arrives in Edo Bay.

The Mitsubishi company is founded, dealing first in shipping and then coal mining.

The Japanese government nationalizes 17 private railway companies.

Nagasaki dockyard opens, with its own ironworks and imported steam hammer.

The first Japanese railroad opens from Tokyo to Yokohama.

The Importance of the Industrial Revolution

The industrial revolution did not happen suddenly and it did not change people's lives overnight. It evolved gradually, as one small, new development led to another, bigger one. Nevertheless, in Europe and elsewhere the events of this period changed an agricultural, rural society into an industrial, urban society. The gradual transformation touched everyone, from noblemen and successful industrialists to peasants and ordinary workers. It affected the lives of men, women, and children, causing significant social as well as economic changes.

Work Changes

Before the industrial revolution, most people in Europe lived on farms and in country villages. In 1800 four out of five Europeans depended on agriculture for their livelihoods. Some farming families regularly moved around the countryside in search of seasonal work. This traditional routine was greatly affected by new agricultural methods which involved less labor. As people moved to the growing towns, their working lives changed dramatically.

A farming family sets out to look for work at haymaking time. Casual workers were expected to have their own tools.

1 *A merchant acted as the entrepreneur throughout the process. First he purchased the raw material, in this case wool.*

2 *The merchant delivered the wool to the working family's cottage. They first sorted, cleaned, and carded the wool.*

Cottage Industry

Before industrialization and even after the invention of power-driven machines, many textiles and other goods were made by country people in their own homes. The whole family worked together in this so-called cottage industry, using traditional skills to make cloth or finished goods. Some merchants provided their working families with spinning wheels and mechanical looms. The sequence of illustrations (right) shows how this domestic system worked.

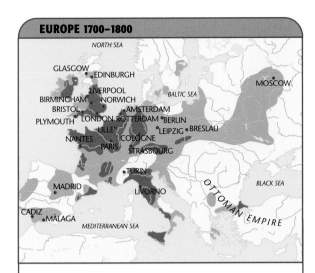

EUROPE 1700–1800

NORTH SEA
GLASGOW
EDINBURGH
MOSCOW
LIVERPOOL
BIRMINGHAM   NORWICH   BALTIC SEA
BRISTOL   AMSTERDAM
PLYMOUTH   LONDON ROTTERDAM BERLIN
LILLE   LEIPZIG   BRESLAU
NANTES   COLOGNE
PARIS   STRASBOURG
TURIN
MADRID   BLACK SEA
LIVORNO
CADIZ   OTTOMAN EMPIRE
MALAGA
MEDITERRANEAN SEA

Population Growth

During the industrial revolution all classes of society generally lived longer and had larger families than previously. Europe's population grew rapidly, from about 140 million in 1750 to 200 million in 1800 and 430 million by the end of the 19th century. Britain's percentage of those figures grew from 5 percent in 1750 to nearly 9 percent in 1900. The map shows the major European centers of population around 1750.

- ● Major centers of population
- Population from 50 to 100 per square mile (1.6 sq km)
- Population over 100 per square mile (1.6 sq km)
- Population less than 50 per square mile (1.6 sq km)

Cities had no mains sewerage before 1850. This brass plaque belonged to a London "nightman," who collected waste from domestic cesspits at night.

The busy city streets were full of life—and noise.

Living Conditions

The industrial revolution led to successful members of the middle and upper classes enjoying more comfortable lives, with better diets and improved health. For working-class people the results were mixed. They were forced to work long hours for low pay, and many of the new jobs were extremely monotonous. Nevertheless, their situation gradually improved during the 19th century, and they too were able to enjoy some of the new products on the market.

3 A spinning wheel was used to twist the raw wool into yarn.

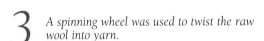

4 Finally, the yarn was woven into fabric. This family did their weaving on a Jacquard loom (invented in 1804), which used punched cards to produce patterns in the cloth.

Westminster Bridge, spanning the Thames River in London, shortly before its completion in 1750.

Ideal Conditions

Conditions in Britain favored the change from an agricultural to an industrial society. The country was politically stable, unified, and free from internal customs duties. It had large deposits of coal and iron, both of which were essential for industrialization. During the 18th century canals were built to connect new industrial centers, adding to new roads and bridges, and transportation was soon to be revolutionized by the introduction of steam railways.

Visitors to the Great Exhibition were amazed by the exhibits and the Crystal Palace that housed them. The building, designed by Joseph Paxton (1803–1865), was almost 2,000 feet (600 m) long, with an iron frame supporting nearly 300,000 panes of glass.

This souvenir box shows the exterior of the Crystal Palace.

These silk shoes were made in London in the 1760s.

Great Britain

The term "Industrial Revolution" was first used in late 19th-century Britain to refer to events in that country that had begun in the previous century. The iron-smelting process was improved, power-driven machinery came into use, canals were built, and factories opened. More British goods were made, and new forms of transportation helped move raw materials and finished products more quickly. By the middle of the 19th century, Victorian Britain was able to stage a Great Exhibition to show the results to its own people and the rest of the world.

London was a bustling trading center. This 19th-century illustration shows St. Katherine's Dock, one of the busiest docks along the Thames.

A Trading Power

Britain was a successful colonial and trading power. Its colonies produced raw materials and themselves became markets for manufactured goods. They helped to stimulate the textile industry, and demand for British goods grew, forcing competing businesses to look for more efficient ways of production to keep prices affordable. Successful entrepreneurs achieved this by developing new machines and factories.

The Great Exhibition

The Great Exhibition of 1851 was designed to show that Britain was the "workshop of the world." The planning committee was headed by Queen Victoria's husband Prince Albert, who opened the exhibition and visited it many times. The Crystal Palace, which contained around 13,000 exhibits, had its own boiler room with steam engines to run the machinery on show.

ENGLAND

1709
Abraham Darby converts a furnace to smelt iron with coke instead of earlier charcoal.

1761
The Bridgewater Canal links the coalmines of Worsley to the city of Manchester.

1774
Matthew Boulton and James Watt open a steam-engine factory in Birmingham.

1785
James Watt's steam engine is first used to power a cotton mill.

1799–1800
The new Combination Acts outlaw trade unions (but are repealed in 1824).

1801
The Act of Union with Ireland creates the United Kingdom of Great Britain and Ireland.

1816
The Leeds–Liverpool Canal is completed.

1851
The Great Exhibition opens on May 1st in Hyde Park, London, and runs until October 11th; more than 6 million people pay to visit the exhibition.

1854
The Crystal Palace, having been taken down and moved from Hyde Park, reopens in Sydenham.

The Factory System

The development of power-driven machines meant that goods could be made more uniformly, more efficiently, and—most important of all to the owner-entrepreneurs—more quickly. Large machines were even more efficient, and they were housed in manufactories, or factories as they came to be known. The textile industry was one of the first sectors to build factories, for its newly developed spinning and weaving machines. Other industries soon followed suit.

Portrait of early industrialist Matthew Boulton (1728–1809).

Organizing Work

Though wages were low, labor was the main production cost in the new factories. Entrepreneurs and factory-owners made sure that workers were properly supervised and disciplined, since they normally now paid for their time rather than the amount of work completed or finished products. New machinery meant that an individual's work became more specialized, since each factory worker concentrated on one single part of the process.

Richard Arkwright (1732–92), who invented a spinning machine that was used in early cotton mills.

Changing the Landscape

Urban centers grew rapidly around the new factories, as working families moved to spreading towns and cities from the country. Since they worked long hours for low pay, traveling to work was out of the question. Dominated by factories, the towns were noisy and dirty. Further out, the growing number of coal mines and ironworks also changed the rural landscape.

Silver tureen made in 1776 at the Birmingham factory of Boulton and John Fothergill.

This 19th-century painting shows a district of Burnley, in Lancashire, dominated by the Lowerhouse print works.

Increased Production

Power-driven machinery meant a greatly increased scale of production, which kept costs down. This interested many different kinds of businessmen, including manufacturers such as Matthew Boulton, who went into partnership with the famous engineer James Watt. Craftsmen such as Josiah Wedgwood (1730–95) also opened factories, so that they could meet the demand that their products created.

THE FACTORY

1769
Josiah Wedgwood opens a pottery-making factory at Etruria, near Stoke-on-Trent in Staffordshire,

1771
Richard Arkwright opens a water-powered mill in Cromford, Derbyshire, helping to pioneer the factory system (see page 18).

1775
Matthew Boulton and James Watt become partners in the steam-engine business.

1779
First steam-powered mills.

1786
Matthew Boulton develops steam-powered coin-minting machinery; Arkwright puts a Watt engine in a cotton mill in Blackfriars, London.

1811–16
During Luddite riots workers destroy factory machines they fear will replace them.

1814
The Times is printed on a steam-driven press.

A Yorkshire miner. His workplace, the colliery, also became more mechanized.

This ornamental vase was made at Wedgwood's large pottery factory.

Spreading Industrialization

Before the existence of factories, textiles and other goods were made in rural homes and small workshops. Many workers were farmers, who added to their income by making products from raw materials provided by a merchant. This cottage industry worked successfully for many, and the earlier methods overlapped with the factory system, which spread across Britain gradually and sporadically.

The Textile Industry

Between the mid-18th and mid-19th century, English factories gradually took over the manufacture of textiles from home workers. Once looms were driven by steam it became much more efficient to group them together in large workrooms. Cotton textiles contributed greatly to the rise of Britain as an industrial nation, as cotton goods became increasingly popular and cheap enough to be afforded by most of the population.

From Wool to Cotton

Britain had developed a thriving wool industry in the late Middle Ages. By the 16th century cotton textiles were being imported, until eventually the British began bringing in raw cotton and spinning and weaving it themselves as a cottage industry. Cotton could be made into a wide variety of fabrics, especially for clothes, as it was comfortable to wear. Technological advances made it possible to mechanize the production of cotton fabric.

Cotton fibers grow out of seed pods of the cotton plant. The fibers can be spun into yarn.

This furnishing fabric of cotton and linen was made in London in 1769. The colors were added using copperplates and woodblocks.

Cotton Processing

The invention of machines revolutionized the cotton industry in Britain. In 1733 John Kay invented the flying shuttle (first used with wool), which increased weaving speed. This meant that more yarn was needed, which spurred the invention of the spinning jenny. Next came the invention of a water-driven spinning machine. These developments, along with the invention of the cotton gin in America, all helped make cotton an important fabric.

INDUSTRIAL ENGLAND

AYR

NORTH SEA

LANCASTER
PRESTON
WIGAN · BLACKBURN
MANCHESTER
CROWE · NOTTINGHAM
DERBY
NORWICH
YARMOUTH
IPSWICH
GLOUCESTER · COLCHESTER
SALISBURY
EXETER · DORCHESTER
ENGLISH CHANNEL

IRISH SEA

BRISTOL CHANNEL

● Cotton ● Silk ● Wool

Spreading Factories

Textile-producing factories spread throughout England during the Industrial Revolution. Wool production was centered on West Yorkshire, the West Country, and East Anglia. The map shows the main manufacturing centers for wool, cotton, and silk. Lancashire also became known for its fustian cloth, a sturdy mixture of cotton and linen.

(see page 18).

TEXTILES

1779
English weaver Samuel Crompton (1753–1827) develops the spinning mule, a cross between the spinning jenny and the water frame (see page 18).

1791
A Manchester mill orders 400 of Edmund Cartwright's power looms, but is burned down by workers fearing for their jobs.

1793
American inventor Eli Whitney (1765–1825) develops a cotton gin that separates seeds from fibers, speeding up production of the raw material.

1801
French inventor Joseph Marie Jacquard develops a loom that can weave cloth with intricate patterns.

1803
William Horrocks improves Cartwright's power loom and makes his machine of iron.

1809
The English Parliament awards Cartwright £10,000 for the benefits to the nation of his power loom.

1856
William Perkin develops the first synthetic dye.

The Power Loom

A clergyman named Edmund Cartwright (1743–1823) changed the history of weaving after visiting Arkwright's Cromford factory in 1784. The following year Cartwright invented his first version of a power loom. The machinery was driven by steam, which speeded the process up enormously. After improvements, the first power loom was soon installed in Cartwright's factory in Doncaster.

This 19th-century engraving shows power looms in use in the weaving room of a textile mill in 1834. A male supervisor oversees the work of female weavers.

Silk

British silk weavers were constantly competing for quality and price with foreign imported goods. But by the 18th century England was the European leader in silk manufacture. Weavers made damasks, velvet, and satins, as well as silk brocades. The main center was at Spitalfields, in east London, where there were 17,000 looms. As power looms became available, silk cloth became even more popular.

This silk twister's wheel, cross, and reeler dates from about 1770. It was turned by hand to twist single filaments of silk into a stronger thread.

This silk dress from the 1860s was dyed with a synthetic mauve. The first synthetic dye was made from coal tar.

The Agricultural Revolution

Beginning in the 17th century, great changes were made to European agriculture, especially in the Low Countries and Britain. Improved methods led to better yields, as leading farmers began treating agriculture as a science. High yields led to low prices, allowing people to buy more manufactured goods and so helping industry. At the same time, fewer farmhands were needed. By 1850 less than a quarter of the British workforce was in agriculture, and many had moved to towns to work in factories.

A Dutch windmill, which was used to pump water from land and reclaim it for farming.

New Machinery

English farmer Jethro Tull (1674–1741) developed two pieces of machinery that contributed to change and progress. The first was a horse-drawn hoe that lifted weeds and turned over soil. The second was a mechanical seed drill, also drawn by horses, which made rows of holes in the soil and dropped seeds in them. The drill sowed three rows at a time and was very productive.

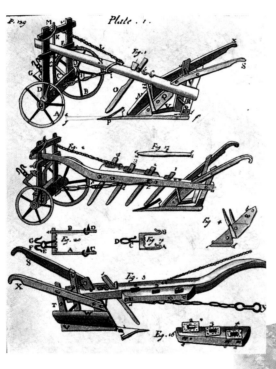

A page from Jethro Tull's book Horse-Hoeing Husbandry, *published in 1731.*

Land Enclosure

The change from open-field strip farming to the rotation system led to more fields being enclosed by fences and hedges. This allowed individual farmers to have complete control over their own fields, working them as units. Farms grew larger, leading to a hierarchy of wealthy landowners, tenant farmers, and landless farm laborers.

Farm laborers, such as this man with his scythe, often moved from farm to farm in search of work.

AGRICULTURE

1701
Jethro Tull develops the seed drill.

1730
Viscount Charles "Turnip" Townshend retires from politics to his Norfolk estate, where he introduces the four-course system.

1755
Robert Bakewell uses selective breeding to produce New Leicester sheep.

1776
Norfolk farming earl Thomas Coke (1752–1852) begins making improvements to farming methods and stockbreeding.

1782
Jethro Tull's seed drill is improved by adding gears.

1783
The first factory for making plows is established in England.

1786
France obtains its first Spanish Merino sheep (officially forbidden from export by Spain); Scottish engineer Andrew Meikle develops a threshing machine.

1836–40
Two General Enclosure Acts allow English landowners to enclose land without referring to Parliament.

Crop Rotation

In the English county of Norfolk, Viscount Townshend introduced a new system of crop rotation that had no fallow year and produced fodder crops. In one field he grew wheat in the first year, clover or ryegrass in the second, oats or barley in the third, and turnips in the fourth year. The clover or ryegrass were grazed by livestock, and the turnips were used as fodder in winter. Manure from the livestock fertilized the fields, which were rotated each year.

Tull's seed drill was a great success, especially since the new system used less seed than old-fashioned sowing by hand.

Feeding the People

The introduction of new rotation methods, machinery, and more animal power increased crop yields significantly. English harvests were good during the first half of the 18th century, and less productive grains such as rye were replaced by higher-yielding wheat or barley. The result was more food for the growing population, including those in the spreading cities.

In the 18th century other European countries tried to increase their crop yields. This illustration shows Frederick the Great encouraging Prussian farmers to grow potatoes.

Stockbreeding

Livestock benefited from the new fodder crops. In the 1760s Leicestershire farmer Robert Bakewell (1725–95) began improving his own animals by selecting breeding stock from those with the best characteristics, such as fine wool or high milk yields. Bakewell successfully bred Leicester sheep, Longhorn cattle, and large white pigs. Others soon followed his example.

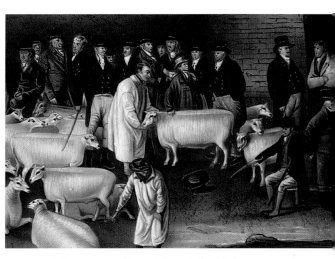

This painting shows Robert Bakewell hiring out his rams to farmers who wanted to improve their own stock.

Steam

English engineer Thomas Savery (1650–1715) invented the first practical steam engine—to pump water from mines—in 1698. Fourteen years later, English blacksmith Thomas Newcomen (1663–1729) developed a more efficient steam pump that had a cylinder fitted with a piston. Since Savery had a wide-ranging patent on his device, Newcomen went into partnership with him.

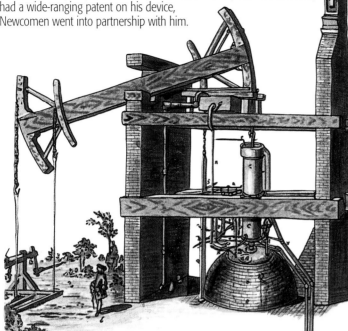

Sources of Power

At the beginning of the industrial revolution the two power sources in addition to muscle power were wind and water. Windmills and waterwheels were useful, but human workers and animals were still needed for many tasks. The invention of the steam engine changed everything, and soon steam—created by burning coal to heat water—was driving machines in factories and mines throughout Britain. At the same time innovative scientists were investigating alternative forms of energy, such as electricity.

Newcomen's steam engine. Steam from the boiler drove a piston in the cylinder, which moved a wooden beam. The other end of the beam operated a pump plunger in the mine shaft.

Horses were used to haul coal, along with mules, oxen, and even dogs.

Human and Animal Power

Many industrial and agricultural activities relied solely on muscle power. In early coal mines, windmills were sometimes used to pump water away. The coal itself was broken loose with picks and loaded into baskets that were carried on the backs of men and women. Alternatively, the coal was put into wooden sledges or wagons that were pushed or hauled to vertical shafts. The coal was raised to the surface using manpower and, later, horsepower.

Up until the 19th century, many children worked long hours. This child is helping to operate a press.

English chemist Sir Humphry Davy (1778–1829) invented the miner's safety lamp in 1815. Its flame was enclosed in a double layer of wire gauze.

Mining Technology

After successful pumping operations, steam engines were soon being used to power windlasses and haul coal to the surface of mines. But it was not until the 19th century that steam engines were used to pull coal along railway tracks. By then rotary ventilation fans had been introduced and special safety lamps were being used by miners to light up the tunnels. These helped cut down explosions caused by naked flames.

A manual windlass was used to lower children and other workers down the mine shaft.

William Watson's book on electricity was published in 1748.

Ponies, women, and children were often used to haul coal along the narrow, low tunnels.

Electricity

In 1745 the Dutch physicist Pieter van Musschenbroek (1692–1761) and the German cleric Ewald Georg von Kleist independently invented a device that could store an electric charge. It was later called a Leyden jar. Two years later, English scientist William Watson (1715–87) increased the capacity of the Leyden jar by coating it with lead foil. These early discoveries led to an understanding of electricity, which would later be used to power many industrial machines.

The glass Leyden jar was sealed with a cork and partly coated with metal foil on its inner and outer surfaces.

Great Inventions

Many of the great inventions of the industrial revolution came about in the textile industry (see pages 12–13), where each practical innovation was aimed at increasing productivity. Water power was largely replaced by steam, and several inventors were involved over a long period in improving the power and efficiency of the steam engine. By the 19th century steam was being used to power railway locomotives, with enormous possibilities for transport.

By turning the wheel on James Hargreaves' spinning jenny, an operator could spin 8 threads on to separate spindles. This number was later doubled and then increased still further.

Combining the Best Features

The 18th-century inventors were practical people, looking to use technology to advance production. Samuel Crompton was a weaver, and his spinning mule was so called because it was a cross between the earlier jenny and frame. The mule produced a strong, fine yarn that could be used in all kinds of textiles and was particularly suited to muslin. Crompton could not afford to pay for a patent and sold his design to Lancashire manufacturers.

Crompton's spinning mule. The first versions were hand-operated, later machines were water-powered, and they were finally driven by steam.

Advancing the Textile Industry

John Kay's flying shuttle greatly increased the amount of cloth weavers could produce, and the next important invention helped supply weavers with more thread. This was the spinning jenny, a hand-operated frame that could spin 8 threads at once. Five years later, Richard Arkwright patented his water frame, a water-powered spinning machine.

Richard Arkwright designed his spinning machine to be powered by water. It was capable of spinning stronger yarn than the jenny.

Right: Arkwright's Cromford cotton mill was built beside a watercourse flowing from the Derwent River. A waterwheel provided power for the factory's water frames.

REVOLUTIONARY INVENTIONS

1709
Coke-burning furnace: Abraham Darby (1678–1717).

1712
Steam engine: Thomas Newcomen (1663–1729).

1733
Flying shuttle: John Kay (1704–64).

1764
Spinning jenny: James Hargreaves (1722–78).

1769
Water frame: Richard Arkwright (1732–92). Improved steam engine: James Watt (1736–1819).

1779
Spinning mule: Samuel Crompton (1753–1827).

1804
Steam locomotive on rails (in an ironworks): Richard Trevithick (1771–1833).

1829
Steam locomotive for public railway: George Stephenson (1781–1848) and Robert Stephenson (1803–59).

A waterwheel drives bellows (or "blowing tubs") that blast air into the furnace to increase the temperature

Workers feed iron ore, coke, and limestone into the top of the furnace.

Molten metal (called pig iron) runs out at the bottom of the furnace. Waste slag is also tapped off.

This 18th-century blast furnace used coke to smelt iron ore, separating the metal from the rock.

Iron Smelting

English ironmaster Abraham Darby wanted to make iron cheaper and easier to produce. Wood, which was needed for making charcoal, was becoming scarce in early 18th-century England. So Darby converted his furnace at Coalbrookdale, Shropshire, to burn coke instead of charcoal. The coke was made by heating coal (which was plentiful) in an airtight oven. The new furnace was ideal for smelting iron.

Steam Locomotives

In 1814 English engineer George Stephenson designed and built a steam locomotive to run on rails and haul coal from mines. Stephenson then constructed the Stockton and Darlington Railway. In 1829 he built an improved locomotive with his son Robert, which won competitive trials and pulled a special train to open the Liverpool and Manchester Railway a year later. The new engine was called *Rocket*.

Watt's steam engine.

The Stephensons' Rocket pulled its own coal and water in a tender. It could travel at 46 kph (28 mph), which was very fast for the time.

Improving Steam Engines

Thomas Newcomen developed his steam engine in 1712 (see page 16). Fifty-seven years later, Scottish engineer James Watt produced an engine that used less coal and produced more power. Watt did this by using a condenser to change steam back into water by cooling. In 1782, Watt improved his own engine by developing a double-action machine, using steam to push a piston both ways

The First Iron Bridge

In 1779 Abraham Darby III, grandson of the ironmaker who devised the coke-fired furnace, built the world's first cast-iron bridge. It still stands today, spanning the River Severn in Shropshire. The bridge's five curved arch ribs were each cast in two halves, and the main parts of the bridge were put together in just three months. Cast iron is made by remelting the pig iron that comes from a furnace and pouring it into casting moulds.

The arch of the famous iron bridge, made of nearly 400 tons of cast iron, spans more than 98 feet (30 m).

Iron and Steel

There were rapid developments in the iron industry from the early 18th century, when coke replaced charcoal in furnaces. Cheaper iron meant that it could be used for many of the machines, pipes, and other parts that were needed in the factories that were springing up in industrial cities. The factories were then able to use iron to manufacture household items that were more practical and cheaper than earlier models in brass or other materials. By the mid-19th century, a new method of producing cheaper steel had also been developed.

Producing Steel

Steel is a refined product of iron and is made by removing impurities from the original metal. In 1740 English clockmaker Benjamin Huntsman used coke as a fuel to remelt iron bars in clay crucibles and make molten steel, which he then cast. Huntsman opened a steelworks in Sheffield, and by 1873 that city was making half the world's steel. The big advantage of steel over iron is its greater strength.

Forging Iron

Scottish engineer James Nasmyth (1808–90) was an expert in machine tools. In 1837 the Great Western Steam Company asked him to help forge some huge iron parts for their new steamship Great Britain. In order to be able to do this, Nasmyth designed and built a powerful steam hammer, which he patented in 1842.

A lump of iron ore, which can be smelted to release the metal.

The Bessemer Process

English engineer Henry Bessemer (1813–98) devised an easier and cheaper way of making steel. In 1856 he developed a converter (turning iron into steel), which was a new kind of furnace lined with a rock called ganister. Air was blown through molten iron in the furnace, and the high temperatures removed impurities and carbon, producing molten steel. Bessemer's new process cut the price of steel in half.

Nasmyth's steam hammer in operation. Steam was used to raise the heavy hammer head, which dropped by its own weight. Extra steam could push the hammer down even harder.

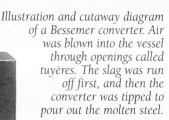

Illustration and cutaway diagram of a Bessemer converter. Air was blown into the vessel through openings called tuyères. The slag was run off first, and then the converter was tipped to pour out the molten steel.

Above. This 19th-century painting shows forge workers hammering hot wrought iron into shape. Wrought iron is softer than cast iron, but less brittle.

Iron was a very useful material for household items. This box iron had a removable slug, which could be heated up in the fireplace.

MINING IN ENGLAND

NORTH SEA

GLASGOW

NEWCASTLE-UPON-TYNE
WORKINGTON • DARLINGTON
STOCKTON

BARROW-IN-FURNES

• LEEDS

IRISH SEA
HOLYHEAD
BIRKENHEAD • SHEFFIELD
• DERBY

WOLVERHAMPTON
IRONBRIDGE •
BIRMINGHAM

SWANSEA GLOUCESTER
• MERTHYR TYDFIL
BRISTOL CHANNEL • BATH

• EXETER
REDRUTH • PLYMOUTH   ENGLISH CHANNEL
PENZANCE

Coal	Tin
Iron	Copper
Lead	

Tapping the Earth's Resources

The map shows the coalfields of England, as well as the mining and smelting sites for important metals. Coal and iron both played a vital role in the Industrial Revolution. Coal was needed as an energy source for steam engines and—as coke—for smelting iron ore (see page 19). By the late 17th century, Britain was producing more than three quarters of the world's coal, from mines spread around the country.

Transportation and Communication

During the first half of the 19th century improved transportation started to changed people's lives. Scottish engineer John McAdam (1756–1836) developed new road surfaces that made travel within and between towns much faster. At the same time steam engines were transforming land and sea transport, with the coming of the railways and the introduction of steamships. Everyday communication was also helped by an improved postal system and by the introduction of an instrument that used electricity to send messages by wire —the telegraph.

The world's first adhesive postage stamp, known as the Penny Black, paid for a letter to be delivered anywhere in Britain.

This Wheatstone telegraph receiver dates from 1842.

Right: French-American transatlantic telegraph.

Steamships

By the 1840s Brunel's propeller-driven iron steamship Great Britain had cabins for 60 first-class passengers and could carry 300 more in lower classes. But the great engineer went on to build a much larger ship, the Great Eastern, which could carry enough coal to steam from Britain to Australia. It was also the only ship big enough to carry the 2,600 miles (4,200 km) of telegraph cable needed to stretch across the Atlantic seabed from Ireland to Newfoundland.

The Telegraph

By 1840 a telegraph system was being used on the railways, speeding up communication. In this system, pulses of electric current caused needles to move and point to individual letters at the receiving end. A system developed by American inventor Samuel Morse speeded things up. The first messages sent along transatlantic cables used Morse code, and they took hours to transmit. But this was still extremely fast international communication for the time.

The Great Eastern's steam engines drove a four-bladed propeller and two giant paddle wheels. There were also six masts of sails.

The excitement of railroad travel is captured in this 1862 painting of Paddington station. Designed by Brunel, the station opened in 1854 as the London terminus of the Great Western Railway.

Two trains on the Liverpool and Manchester Railway show closed, more comfortable first-class carriages (above, with luggage on top), and a second-class service open to the elements.

THE RAILROAD SYSTEM

Major railroad

NEWCASTLE ON TYNE

NORTH SEA

MANCHESTER

LIVERPOOL SHEFFIELD

DERBY

IRISH SEA

CAMBRIDGE

LONDON

ENGLISH CHANNEL

All Aboard!

The new railroads changed the way people of all classes thought about travel. There were usually three classes of travel, with a great difference in comfort between them. The London to Brighton railroad line opened in 1841, and over the next three decades other seaside resorts grew up along the British coast. The success of the railroads kept prices down, and even working-class passengers could afford a day trip to the seaside.

Expanding Network

The Liverpool and Manchester Railway, opened in 1830, was the first to offer passenger services with a regular timetable. The venture was so successful that it caused an enormous railway-building boom. By 1850, there were nearly 6,300 miles (10,000 km) of railroad track in Britain. The tracks all had a standard gauge of 4 feet 8½ inches (1.44 m).

The Commercial Revolution

In Britain the industrial revolution was supported by a successful banking system, including the Bank of England and private financiers. Commerce had previously been strongly regulated under the system of mercantilism that encouraged exports and the establishment of overseas colonies. In the 18th century this was replaced by a capitalist system in which bankers, merchants, and industrialists became more important than landowners. Commercial markets grew wider and became more secure.

This Great Iron Chest was used from the beginning of the 18th century for the safekeeping of bills in the Bank of England.

Economic Philosophy

Adam Smith is often regarded as the founder of modern economics. He argued for capitalism, the economic system based on private ownership of the means of production and a free competitive market. Smith maintained that governments should adopt a laissez-faire attitude to the economy, allowing individuals to follow their business interests without interference. He believed that, in order to make money, manufacturers produce things that consumers want to buy, creating wealth and an expanding economy.

Scottish economist and philosopher Adam Smith (1723–90).

Bank of England

The Bank of England was set up by a group of London merchants to raise funds for the British government to finance war in the Low Countries. During the 18th century it developed into a commercial bank, taking deposits and issuing banknotes, which at first were partially printed with cashiers making out the exact sum involved. In 1793 the Bank issued its printed £5 note, which still had to be signed by hand by a Bank cashier.

Workers were strictly supervised at the Bank of England's press in Threadneedle Street, which started printing its own banknotes in 1808. The notes were printed from engraved copper plates.

BANKING AND TRADE

1694
Foundation of the Bank of England.

1765
Sampson Lloyd and John Taylor set up a private banking business in Birmingham, England— Lloyds Bank.

1773
A group of brokers establish a Stock Exchange in London's Threadneedle Street.

1776
Publication of An Inquiry into the Nature and Causes of the Wealth of Nations *by Adam Smith.*

1792
The New York Stock Exchange is established.

1826
In Britain the Country Bankers Act allows the establishment of joint-stock banks more than 65 miles (100 km) from London.

1844
The Bank Charter Act recognizes the Bank of England as Britain's central banknote-issuing authority.

Private Banking

By the late 17th century some goldsmiths, merchants, and legal clerks offered their own financial and banking services in London. They accepted deposits of money, made loans, and exchanged foreign coins. Any of their customers could also instruct the financier to pay money from their account to another person. In the British provinces, so-called "country banks" could not compete with the Bank of England until restrictions on them were lifted in 1826.

This handwritten document of 1725 is addressed to a London goldsmith. It requests a payment of £70 to be made to a named individual, in the same way as a modern check would do.

Growing Businesses

The industrial revolution stimulated manufacturing, which helped all kinds of businesses to grow. Company owners sold shares in their businesses to shareholders, and the resulting capital allowed small specialist companies to expand into wider areas. For further expansion, manufacturers raised long-term capital by mortgaging factory buildings and machinery to banks

This 18th-century engraving shows the Royal Exchange in London, built in 1669, where merchants met to conduct business.

Belgium and France

Newly independent Belgium, under King Leopold I (whose niece became Britain's Queen Victoria six years after his accession), was quick to follow Britain in its move toward industrialization. This was particularly evident in the French-speaking southern regions of the country. France itself also expanded its economy, especially after 1852, and both countries developed transportation systems to move people, raw materials, and the new goods produced. This helped trade between the two countries and their neighbors.

This Belgian coin shows King Leopold II, during whose reign (1865–1909) there was great colonial expansion.

Belgian Industry

Early in the 19th century industry developed fast in the southern Belgian region of French-speaking Wallonia, while Dutch-speaking Flanders remained largely agricultural. The coal mines of the Borinage region increased production, and iron and steel developed around Charleroi. The Belgian government encouraged a system of free private enterprise, and Belgian banks invested heavily in Walloon industry.

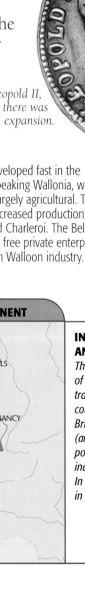

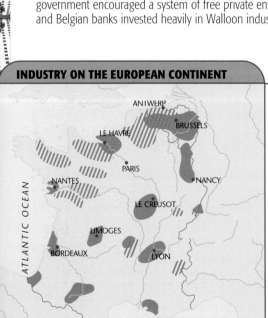

INDUSTRY ON THE EUROPEAN CONTINENT

ANTWERP
BRUSSELS
LE HAVRE
PARIS
NANTES
NANCY
LE CREUSOT
LIMOGES
BORDEAUX
LYON
ATLANTIC OCEAN

INDUSTRY IN FRANCE AND BELGIUM

The map shows how the face of France and Belgium was transformed by industry during the course of the 19th century. As in Britain, the presence of coalfields (and their usefulness for steam power) tended to further the industrialization of a region. In France, industry developed most in the north and east.

■ Heavy industry

/// Major textile manufacturing

The 16th-century Maison du Roi ("King's House") in central Brussels was restored in the 1870s.

New Transport Links

Belgium developed an excellent network of roads, railroads, and canals, connecting the industrial south with Brussels and, most importantly, the port of Antwerp. The Charleroi–Brussels Canal was part of a waterway system that linked rivers. From the outset the Belgian railroads were state-owned, and in 1843 a line connected Antwerp to Cologne, helping Belgian exports.

View of the 1900 Exposition Universelle in Paris. It lasted 7 months and attracted more than 50 million visitors.

BELGIUM AND FRANCE

1803
The coal mines of the Borinage region (part of France, later Belgium) are updated with conveyor belts, causing an increase in coal output.

1827–32
Building of the Charleroi–Brussels Canal. 1830 The major European powers of Austria, Britain, France, Prussia and Russia recognize Belgian independence.

1835
The Banque de Belgique is founded by Belgian liberals; the first Belgian railway links Brussels with Mechelen.

1837
First public railway in France opens between Paris and Saint Germain.

1844
Belgium makes a favorable trade agreement with Germany.

1852
Louis Napoleon Bonaparte (nephew of Napoleon I) declares himself emperor of France and establishes the Second Empire.

1853–70
Georges-Eugène Haussmann is prefect of the French department of Seine and redesigns Paris with wide, straight avenues.

1869–87
Building of the Bon Marché department store in Paris.

1870–71
France is defeated in the Franco-Prussian War and loses most of Alsace and part of Lorraine.

Expositions Universelles

Universal Expositions (or World's Fairs) helped Parisians and others celebrate French industrial expansion. The first was held in Paris in 1855, just four years after London's Great Exhibition (see page 9). The 6-month Exposition showcased French wine production and attracted 4.5 million visitors.

There were further successful fairs in 1867, 1878, and 1889, when the main symbol was the newly completed Eiffel Tower. Several bridges and railway stations were built specially for the 1900 Exposition.

A 19th-century textile factory in Mulhouse, a manufacturing center in the Alsace region.

The Second Empire

French industrial production doubled during the period of its Second Empire (1852–70). French industry turned to steam power, as many more railway tracks were laid so that the network covered the whole country. The textile industry grew, and cotton manufacture was second only to Britain. Great French investment banks were founded, and successful shops grew into grand department stores in Paris. The capital itself was renovated and redesigned by the administrator Georges-Eugène Haussmann.

Germany

By the mid-19th century, Germany's growing railroads were causing an increased demand for coal and iron. North German industrial centers expanded, and Prussia's victory over France and unification in 1871 led to the foundation of large, successful companies. Though there was a worldwide depression just two years later, more than four-fifths of the new German firms survived. Adding to steel-making and engineering, German scientists, inventors, and industrialists helped their country dominate the new chemical and electrical industries.

Founder Years

The period 1871–73 in Germany is known as the Gründerjahre ("founder years"), because so many enterprises were founded after unification. More than 850 joint-stock companies were established, requiring more investment in two years than had been made in the previous two decades. Much of this came from investment banks that were created to finance industry rather than provide credit for individuals.

The Krupp Factory

Alfred Krupp (1812–87) took over his father's cast-steel factory in Essen at the age of 14. The family firm was the first on the European continent to introduce the Bessemer process (see page 20), making railway tracks and axles. In 1851 the factory produced a cast-steel cannon that was shown at the Great Exhibition in London (see page 8). This led to Krupp becoming Europe's leading arms manufacturer, and the success of its guns in the Franco-Prussian War led to the nickname "arsenal of the empire."

Workers at the Krupp steelworks use a massive steam hammer to forge ingots.

One of Krupp's huge cannons on exhibition in 1867.

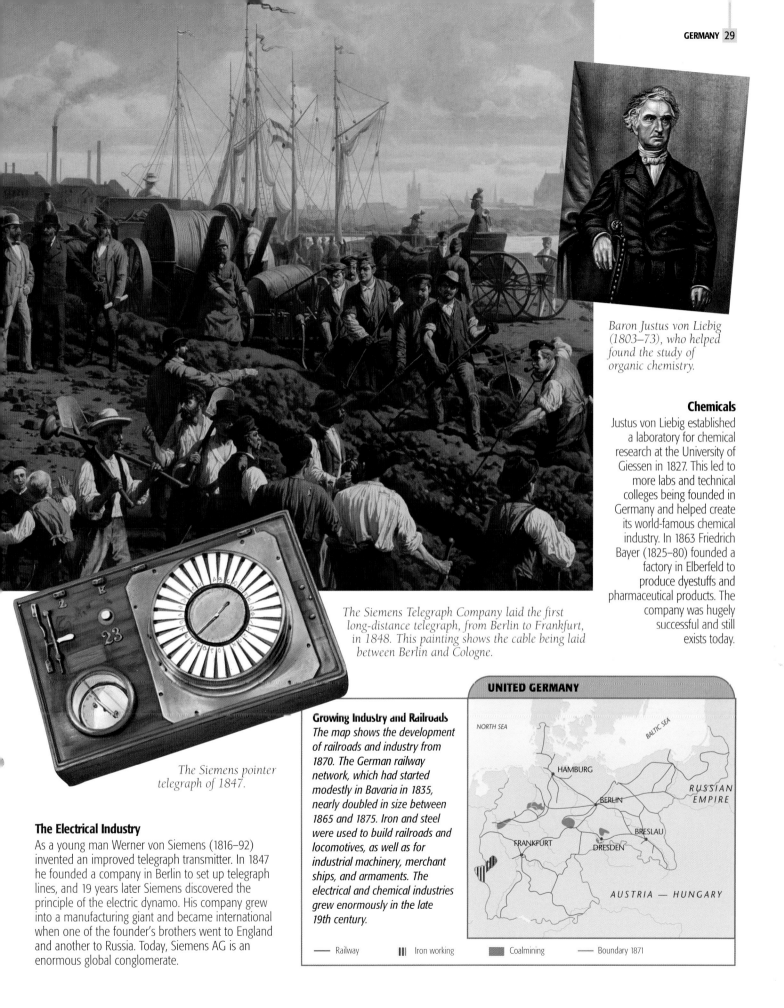

Baron Justus von Liebig (1803–73), who helped found the study of organic chemistry.

Chemicals

Justus von Liebig established a laboratory for chemical research at the University of Giessen in 1827. This led to more labs and technical colleges being founded in Germany and helped create its world-famous chemical industry. In 1863 Friedrich Bayer (1825–80) founded a factory in Elberfeld to produce dyestuffs and pharmaceutical products. The company was hugely successful and still exists today.

The Siemens Telegraph Company laid the first long-distance telegraph, from Berlin to Frankfurt, in 1848. This painting shows the cable being laid between Berlin and Cologne.

The Siemens pointer telegraph of 1847.

The Electrical Industry

As a young man Werner von Siemens (1816–92) invented an improved telegraph transmitter. In 1847 he founded a company in Berlin to set up telegraph lines, and 19 years later Siemens discovered the principle of the electric dynamo. His company grew into a manufacturing giant and became international when one of the founder's brothers went to England and another to Russia. Today, Siemens AG is an enormous global conglomerate.

Growing Industry and Railroads

The map shows the development of railroads and industry from 1870. The German railway network, which had started modestly in Bavaria in 1835, nearly doubled in size between 1865 and 1875. Iron and steel were used to build railroads and locomotives, as well as for industrial machinery, merchant ships, and armaments. The electrical and chemical industries grew enormously in the late 19th century.

UNITED GERMANY

NORTH SEA
BALTIC SEA
HAMBURG
BERLIN
RUSSIAN EMPIRE
FRANKFURT
BRESLAU
DRESDEN
AUSTRIA — HUNGARY

— Railway ||| Iron working ▬ Coalmining — Boundary 1871

The United States of America

The transformation of the United States (and Germany) into industrial nations is sometimes known as the second industrial revolution. In the US, developments largely took place after the end of the Civil War in 1865. Coal, iron, and steel production increased, railroads were built across the continent, factories opened, and industry advanced much faster than agriculture. By the end of the 19th century, the US had grown into the world's leading producer of many industrial products.

Whitney's cotton gin (short for "engine") revolutionized the cotton industry in the US and Europe.

THE UNITED STATES

A Land Rich in Natural Resources

An abundance of raw materials was an important factor in the industrial growth of the United States. As in Britain, coal was a vital resource: in 1800 the US produced 98,000 tons of coal; by 1850 the figure was 7.6 million tons, and by 1900 245 million tons. Metals were mined, including all-important iron, as well as oil and gas. The growing railroad network made it easier to transport materials.

■ Coal   ● Oil and gas
● Iron   ● Cotton

Cotton

After the American inventor Eli Whitney developed a cotton gin to separate seeds from fibers quickly and efficiently, the United States became the world's leading cotton grower. The slave population grew in the south to pick and gin cotton, contributing to the causes of the Civil War. In 1860 agricultural goods still made up more than two-thirds of US exports. After 1865, large numbers of cotton mills sprang up in the south to make cotton cloth.

This distinctive kind of American locomotive was first built in Philadelphia in 1837.

An early Singer sewing machine. I.M. Singer & Co. was established in New York in 1851, and soon became the most famous manufacturer of sewing machines.

Iron and Steel

English colonists had brought iron-making skills and techniques with them to the New World. By 1864 the Bessemer process (see page 20) was being used in the United States to turn iron into steel. This development supplied the material that helped the growth of railroads and manufacturing industries. In 1873, Andrew Carnegie established the first large-scale US steel plant in Braddock, Pennsylvania. By the early 20th century, the US was producing more steel than Germany or Britain.

Scottish-born Andrew Carnegie (1835–1919) (left) emigrated with his family at the age of 12. He made his fortune in steel manufacture and became a noted philanthropist.

The First Oil Wells

When the news spread that Edwin Drake had struck oil, prospectors rushed to Pennsylvania. Oil wells soon sprang up near Titusville along a river that came to be known as Oil Creek, and boom towns were founded. At first the new oil industry was chaotic, but businessmen such as John D. Rockefeller brought order to the production, refining, and distribution of "black gold."

Portrait of John Davison Rockefeller (1839–1937), who formed the hugely successful Standard Oil Company in 1870.

Wooden derricks in the Oil Creek region of Pennsylvania. In 1861 the Phillips well (on the right) produced 4,000 barrels of oil a day.

INDUSTRY IN THE UNITED STATES

1817
The New York Stock & Exchange Board (later Stock Exchange) is established.

1830
The first US passenger train steams along a local line in South Carolina.

1839
Connecticut inventor Charles Goodyear discovers vulcanization, a process used to make rubber stronger.

1859
Edwin Drake (1819–80) strikes oil near Titusville, Pennsylvania.

1861–65
The American Civil War between the northern Union and the southern Confederacy.

1869
Railway lines meet at Promontory, Utah, to complete the first continuous track across the US.

1876
Alexander Graham Bell displays his telephone at Philadelphia's Centennial Exhibition.

1879
Thomas Edison (1847–1931) invents the light bulb.

1882
Electric lighting illuminates New York City; John D. Rockefeller controls the US oil-refinery business.

1892
Andrew Carnegie combines three of his firms and forms the Carnegie Steel Company.

Russia

At the start of the second half of the 19th century, the Russian tsar and leading figures in his empire set about trying to catch up with progress made by the leading European countries. They introduced a program of industrialization, fuelled as elsewhere by coal and also by oil, and including an expanding railroad network. But in Russia discontent grew among workers in the growing cities, and the empire's industrial revolution soon led to strikes and the 1917 Bolshevik revolution.

Coal miners worked long hours in harsh conditions. These men are watched over by armed soldiers as they work.

Trans-Siberian Railway

In 1889 Count Witte (then in the Ministry of Communications) set up a railway department in the Ministry of Finance. Two years later the first track was laid to open the cold, vast region of Siberia to Muscovites and others. By 1904 the track was complete all the way from Moscow to Vladivostok, on the Pacific coast, a distance of more than 5,600 miles (9,000 km). It helped open up Siberia for settlement and industry.

Social and Economic Change

Following the freeing of the serfs, Russian industrialization accelerated during the last decades of the 19th century. A new class of businessmen rapidly developed, but there were still great difficulties for ordinary people as old-fashioned agricultural methods continued while modern factories were coming into operation. Rapid changes continued, as French and Belgian capital was invested in the steel industry, the British invested in Russian oil (see opposite), and Germany in electricity.

A postcard of Vladivostok, which was founded as a Russian naval port in 1860.

Postage stamp of 1922 showing a gushing Baku oil well.

Portrait of finance minister Count Witte (1849–1915), who helped modernize the empire, expanding the railroads and developing industry.

MINING

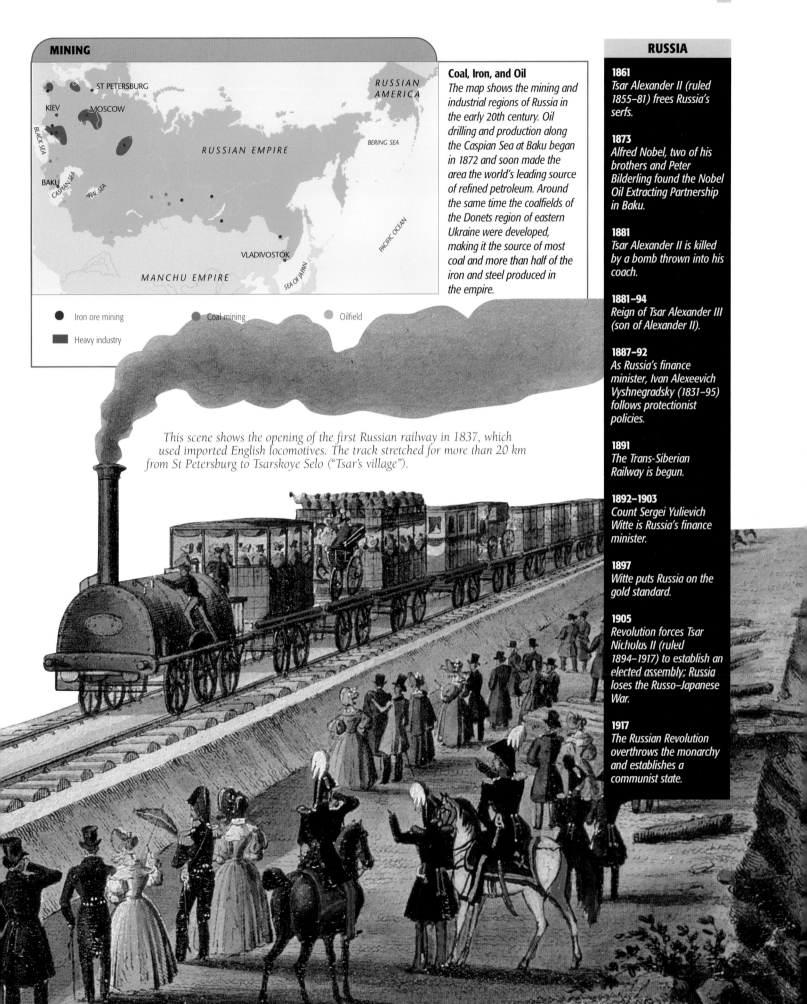

ST PETERSBURG
KIEV
MOSCOW
BLACK SEA
BAKU
CASPIAN SEA
ARAL SEA
RUSSIAN EMPIRE
RUSSIAN AMERICA
BERING SEA
PACIFIC OCEAN
VLADIVOSTOK
SEA OF JAPAN
MANCHU EMPIRE

● Iron ore mining   ● Coal mining   ● Oilfield
■ Heavy industry

Coal, Iron, and Oil

The map shows the mining and industrial regions of Russia in the early 20th century. Oil drilling and production along the Caspian Sea at Baku began in 1872 and soon made the area the world's leading source of refined petroleum. Around the same time the coalfields of the Donets region of eastern Ukraine were developed, making it the source of most coal and more than half of the iron and steel produced in the empire.

This scene shows the opening of the first Russian railway in 1837, which used imported English locomotives. The track stretched for more than 20 km from St Petersburg to Tsarskoye Selo ("Tsar's village").

RUSSIA

1861
Tsar Alexander II (ruled 1855–81) frees Russia's serfs.

1873
Alfred Nobel, two of his brothers and Peter Bilderling found the Nobel Oil Extracting Partnership in Baku.

1881
Tsar Alexander II is killed by a bomb thrown into his coach.

1881–94
Reign of Tsar Alexander III (son of Alexander II).

1887–92
As Russia's finance minister, Ivan Alexeevich Vyshnegradsky (1831–95) follows protectionist policies.

1891
The Trans-Siberian Railway is begun.

1892–1903
Count Sergei Yulievich Witte is Russia's finance minister.

1897
Witte puts Russia on the gold standard.

1905
Revolution forces Tsar Nicholas II (ruled 1894–1917) to establish an elected assembly; Russia loses the Russo–Japanese War.

1917
The Russian Revolution overthrows the monarchy and establishes a communist state.

Japan

Japan was an isolated country until international trade links were forcefully opened during the mid-19th century. This was quickly followed by a revolution that put an end to the old feudal system. These changes led to the industrialization of Japan, as politicians and businessmen learned European methods and imported machinery. The growing national industries were sold to private companies, some of which quickly grew into large enterprises. The new Japanese leadership also developed its military force, building naval shipyards and modernizing weapons.

Mihorabashi railway station. The advanced Japanese rail system and a nationwide telegraph network contributed to the country's industrial modernization.

Commodore Matthew Calbraith Perry (1794–1858) meeting a representative of the Japanese emperor.

Open for Trade

Four US Navy warships arrived in Edo (now Tokyo) Bay in 1853, under the command of Commodore Perry. The commodore carried a letter from the US president to the Japanese emperor, asking Japan to open its ports to international trade. This was not immediately successful, but Perry returned a year later with eight ships and negotiations then began. A treaty was soon signed, opening two (and later, more) Japanese ports.

INDUSTRIAL JAPAN

Railway

Industrial areas

HOKKAIDO

SEA OF JAPAN

HONSHU

SHIKOKU

KYUSHU

PACIFIC OCEAN

Rise of Industry

Traditional industries—such as ceramics, textiles, and silk manufacture—were expanded and modernized. During the period 1868–98, exports multiplied tenfold, though imports grew even faster. From 1890, the emphasis switched to heavy industry, including manufacturing, machine-building, shipbuilding, iron and steel, and the chemical industry. This was helped by the expanding railroad network. The map shows the main centers.

Textiles

Traditional Japanese textile manufacture was gradually mechanized. Spinning mules were imported from Britain and France, and in 1883 a steam-powered cotton-spinning factory opened in Osaka. Some of the growing factories included dormitories and hospitals for workers, and schools for their children. By the end of the Meiji era, factory-produced cotton and silk had become major Japanese exports.

The Meiji Era

The end of feudal rule in Japan was brought about by a non-violent revolution known as the Meiji Restoration (1866–1868). Though this nominally returned full authority to the emperor, the political leaders held real power and set about modernizing industry, strengthening the military, and enriching the nation. They achieved this by copying the successful methods adopted in Europe and North America, and by importing expensive machinery for their new factories.

A Japanese helmet of the Meiji era. Samurai swords were replaced by European-style rifles. In 1894–1895 a war with China gained Japanese control of Formosa (now Taiwan), southern Manchuria, and Korea.

JAPAN

1853
On July 8, US Commodore Perry's squadron arrives in Edo Bay, Japan.

1856–61
Townsend Harris (1804–78) serves as the first US consul general to Japan.

1861
Nagasaki dockyard opens, with its own ironworks and imported steam hammer.

1867
Japanese delegates at the Universal Exposition in Paris visit French factories to learn about new technology.

1868–1912
The Meiji ("enlightened rule") era during which Emperor Mutsuhito reigns.

1870
The Mitsubishi company is founded, dealing first in shipping and then coal mining.

1871
Feudalism is declared abolished; 300 former fiefs become 72 prefectures and 3 metropolitan districts.

1872
The first Japanese railway opens from Tokyo to Yokohama.

1885
The Imperial College of Engineering merges with Tokyo University.

1906
The Japanese government nationalizes 17 private railway companies.

Japanese factory-workers produced silk to compete in export markets with China. By the 1870s many human-powered drive-wheels had been replaced by steam power.

Painting of 1834 of the German Ruhr valley town of Burg Wetter, where factories were built around the medieval castle.

Moving to Town

During the early period of the Industrial Revolution some workers migrated according to the seasons. They stayed in the country during the harvest season, and moved to town when they needed other work. Many stayed in town permanently, however, attracted by the offer of constant work in the new factories. Some towns specialized in one form of industry: there were "mill towns" and "coke towns," and even "company towns" as individual firms expanded.

City Streets

As carriages and other forms of transportation improved, better roadways were needed. Cobbled and stone-surfaced streets were made smoother, and pavements were added for pedestrians. In Paris, there were 160 miles (260 km) of pavements by 1848. Later in the century, many streets were surfaced with asphalt. By this time, roads were lit at night. Gas lighting was introduced in London in 1807, Baltimore in 1816, and Paris in 1820. Electric lighting began to take over in the 1880s.

The two-wheeled hansom cab was a popular method of urban transportation from the 1830s.

Left: In this cartoon, some Londoners marvel at the new gas lighting, while others are more sceptical.

Drains and Sewers

Before the problems of waste removal were tackled in the mid-19th century, streets were dirty and smelly. Disease was rife in congested cities, where cholera, typhus, and smallpox were all big killers. In the 1850s, proper sewerage and drainage systems were dug beneath the streets of Paris and London. This was an enormous undertaking and an impressive engineering achievement, using the latest technology. By 1878 the Parisian sewer system was 375 miles (600 km) long.

Urbanization

Industrialization led to urban growth, which occurred most rapidly in the birthplace of the industrial revolution —Britain. By the beginning of the 19th century 24 percent of the British population was already living in towns of 10,000 or more people. In the rest of Europe the figure was less than 10 percent. The new town-dwellers faced problems of poor housing, water supplies, and sanitation, leading to an urgent need for modernization and social planning.

Sandstone tunnels were dug beneath the streets of Paris. They contained storm drains, a main sewer with sidewalks, iron mains pipes for drinking water, and a separate supply of non-drinkable water. Some sections were even built for tourists, who were carried at first by suspended carts and later by carriage.

Chicago streets were paved with tarred pine blocks in 1859. The flat surface of blocks was covered with pitch and gravel.

Growing Cities

The world's cities grew bigger as railroads made it possible for wealthier people to move further out to the suburbs. Ordinary workers stayed near their place of work, around the city center, and poverty led to many of these areas turning into slums. In more prosperous districts buildings grew taller. The use of steel for constructing the framework of tall buildings was introduced in Chicago in the 1880s and soon spread throughout North America.

By 1870 the streets of Paris had been widened, helping the movement of horse-drawn omnibuses and trams. These larger, faster vehicles made pedestrian pavements even more important. Buildings grew taller as the age of the Parisian department store began.

City Life

Growing industrial cities presented middle-class professional people and working-class wage earners with enormous opportunities. But there were great contrasts between the different classes of society. Life was certainly hard for those with little money, and many slid into poverty. Back-to-back terraced houses with poor sanitation offered very little space or privacy to large families. Work was often hard to find, and travel was expensive, so working-class people were forced to live near their place of work.

Hazards

As well as facing the problems of inadequate housing and poor sanitation, city-dwellers were constantly at the mercy of fire. Firefighters existed, but there was no coordination between different brigades in cities. There were so many fires in London that insurance companies set up a Fire Engine Establishment with 19 fire stations in 1833, and the Metropolitan (later London) Fire Brigade was formed in 1865. Insurance was of little interest to the poor, who could not afford it and owned no property.

A horse-drawn steam-pump fire engine rushes to a fire in New York.

Rich and Poor

The urban middle class of wealthy merchants, bankers, and professional people lived in pleasantly comfortable, large homes. Many rooms had a coal fireplace, which led to smoke pollution throughout the city. Working-class people lived in much simpler, smaller houses. But life for the poor of the city was dreadful. Many lived in overcrowded slums, where small houses were dirty and unheated.

Fifth Avenue, New York, in 1883, just after the completion of the Vanderbilt mansion.

A narrow alley separates these workers' houses in London.

Street Children

In mid 19th-century Britain average life expectancy was 40 for men and 42 for women. Poor people often died much younger, leaving homeless orphans to roam the streets. Some found work as street sellers, crossing-sweepers, or deliverers, but others slipped into a life of petty crime. They picked pockets in busy streets, stole food when they could, and spent their nights in outhouses or doorways.

Flower sellers earned a paltry sum working the streets of Victorian London.

Contrasts

The busy streets of Victorian cities such as London were full of contrasts. Outside the neat stores of grocers, butchers, bakers, and other shopkeepers, many tradesmen conducted their business and did their selling on the street itself. Pavements were narrow, if they existed at all, and horse-drawn carts, carriages, and cabs fought their way past each other.

The streets of Victorian London were full of life, as merchants, shopkeepers, and artisans went about their daily business.

THE CITY

1842
Aqueduct opens in New York to increase water available to firefighters; English social reformer Anthony Ashley Cooper pushes through a bill that bars women and children under 10 from working in coal mines.

1844
The charitable Ragged School Union is founded in London to provide basic education for the poor.

1847
Another of Cooper's bills shortens the working day in textile mills to 10 hours.

1848
Cholera epidemic in Britain.

1862
American philanthropist George Peabody's trust founds its first block of buildings in London for the "poor and needy."

1865
Volunteer firefighters in New York City are replaced by the professional Metropolitan Fire Department.

1876–81
German physician Robert Koch discovers the anthrax bacterium, and French scientist Louis Pasteur develops an anthrax vaccine.

1880
A new wave of immigrants arrives in the US and most move straight to cities.

1884–85
British Royal Commission looks into the housing of the working classes.

1888
he London Whitechapel murders are committed by "Jack the Ripper."

1901
Queen Victoria dies.

Working Families

Industrialization and the growth of cities had a great impact on the family life of working-class people. The place of work moved away from the home to the factory, where in many cases men, women, and children had to work long hours in order to make ends meet. Home life suffered as women were faced with the burden of factory work being followed by domestic chores and childcare. Other women went into domestic service in middle-class households, where life was very different. Few middle-class women were required to work in paid employment.

The family was seen as central to the middle-class ideal of a stable life. All family members were expected to try and better themselves.

Tokens such as this were issued to factory workers to buy food.

The Working Classes

The hierarchical structure of society into upper, middle, and lower or working classes was reinforced by the Industrial Revolution. Skilled craftsmen, shopkeepers, and higher domestic servants were at the upper end of the working class, and unskilled laborers at the lower. Generally the lower working classes had no education. Industrialization also created a new class of manual worker—the machine-minder, who received a short period of training and became familiar with one part of a factory process.

Child Labor

Many children were sent to work at a very young age, and had to put in long hours. In the British textile industry of 1861, nearly a fifth of the workforce was under 15. In mines, the figure was 12 percent. Small children were used for cleaning machinery, such as removing fluff from under power looms. Since the machines were kept running, it was dangerous work. In other factories, children worked as assistants to adult machine-minders.

This unfortunate boy got his foot caught in machinery.

Factory Hours

Factory conditions were often hard, and hours were always long. Many people, including children, worked 16 hours a day. In 1833 the British government recommended changes in the textile industry: 9–11 year olds' hours were cut to 8 a day, and under-18s to 12 a day. Things were not much better for a whole class of domestic servants. Many worked 80 hours a week for very little pay, but they had the advantage of being well fed and were given clothing and shelter.

In this illustration of 1868, men, women and children make their way home after a long day's work at a Massachusetts textile factory.

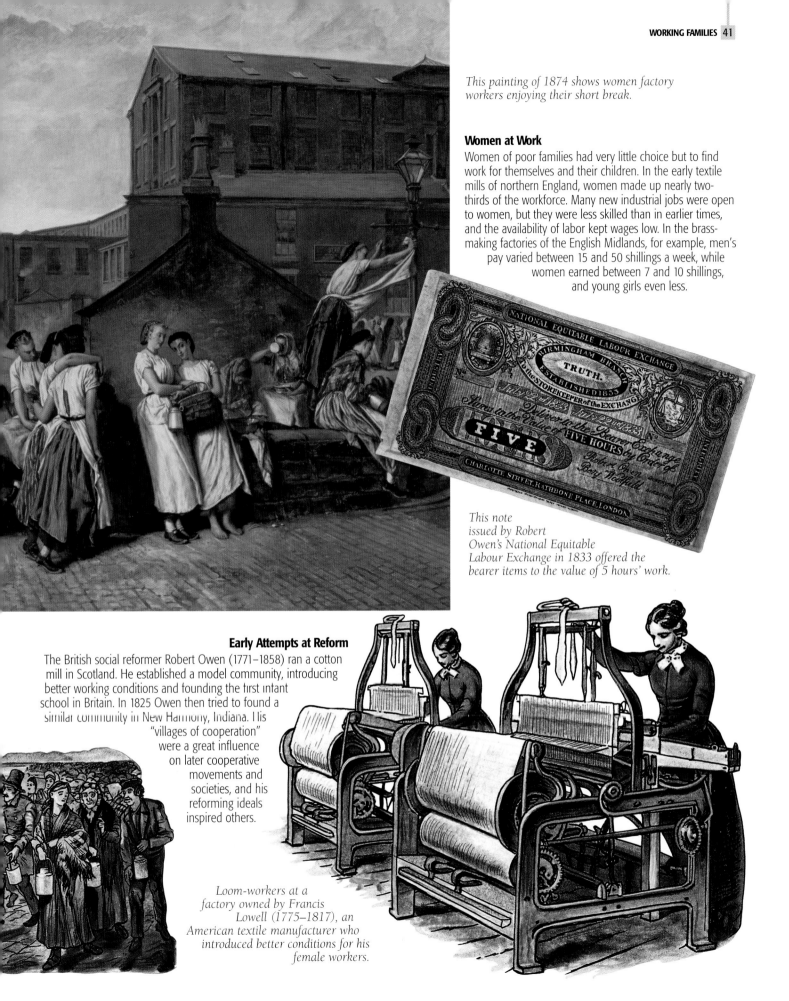

This painting of 1874 shows women factory workers enjoying their short break.

Women at Work

Women of poor families had very little choice but to find work for themselves and their children. In the early textile mills of northern England, women made up nearly two-thirds of the workforce. Many new industrial jobs were open to women, but they were less skilled than in earlier times, and the availability of labor kept wages low. In the brass-making factories of the English Midlands, for example, men's pay varied between 15 and 50 shillings a week, while women earned between 7 and 10 shillings, and young girls even less.

This note issued by Robert Owen's National Equitable Labour Exchange in 1833 offered the bearer items to the value of 5 hours' work.

Early Attempts at Reform

The British social reformer Robert Owen (1771–1858) ran a cotton mill in Scotland. He established a model community, introducing better working conditions and founding the first infant school in Britain. In 1825 Owen then tried to found a similar community in New Harmony, Indiana. His "villages of cooperation" were a great influence on later cooperative movements and societies, and his reforming ideals inspired others.

Loom-workers at a factory owned by Francis Lowell (1775–1817), an American textile manufacturer who introduced better conditions for his female workers.

Trade Unions and Social Reform

It was some time after the great changes brought about by the Industrial Revolution that workers began to organize themselves into useful groups. The first aim was to improve pay and conditions, and this was largely achieved by the growing labor movement. Social reformers and political revolutionaries put forward theories as to how the so-called class conflict could be resolved. In practice, trade unionists improved their members' working lives, and liberal-minded politicians changed laws to help working-class families and their children's education.

Some workers believed that new machinery was ruining the labor market. In the early 19th century Luddites attacked textile factories in the north of England.

The Labor Movement

The dramatic changes in ordinary people's working lives caused by industrialization led to a movement by groups of workers to improve their economic position. New laws and rights were needed, because factory owners and other employers abused the plentiful labor market by offering low pay and poor conditions. Workers realized that they could use collective action and, if necessary, strikes as weapons, while employers fell back on old-fashioned laws to protect their interests.

Education

Children's working conditions and education were linked in 19th-century Britain. Factory Acts reduced working hours, and the Elementary Education Act of 1870 set up school boards across the country. Boards were free to decide whether education was compulsory from ages 5 to 10 in their district, but this was enforced nationally in 1880. At first board schools cost parents a few pence each week, encouraging many to keep their children at work. Fees were generally abolished in 1891.

A schoolchild's writing slate, which could be wiped clean and used over and over again.

Social Reform

For some reformers the labor movement was part of a class struggle that they saw leading to a workers' revolution. The German philosopher Karl Marx and social scientist Friedrich Engels believed that the industrial proletariat (or wage-earning workers) would inevitably win their struggle with the capitalist bourgeoisie (owner-employers) and create a new society free of class conflict and oppression. These ideas influenced thinkers and politicians all over the world.

Karl Marx (1818–83) was a leading figure in the First International. His revolutionary theories encouraged socialists and communists.

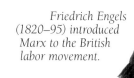

Friedrich Engels (1820–95) introduced Marx to the British labor movement.

Membership card of the International Working Men's Association (or First International), an organization of labor groups founded in London in 1864.

Trade Unions

Workers formed trade unions in order to use their bargaining power as a group, which was much greater than that of individuals. In Britain early unions of the 1850s faced strong opposition from employers, who refused to recognize them. Unions themselves were separate until the Trades Union Congress of 1868 formed a national organization. The TUC was made up of unions of skilled workers until 1889, when it started to accept general unions.

Membership certificate of the first successful national trade union, the Amalgamated Society of Engineers, formed in 1851.

LABOR MOVEMENT

1848
Publication of the Communist Manifesto by Marx and Engels.

1867
First volume of Marx's Das Kapital is published.

1868
First meeting of the Trades Union Congress (TUC) takes place in Manchester.

1869
The first US national workers' organization, the Noble Order of the Knights of Labor, is founded in Philadelphia.

1871
The Trade Union Act recognizes unions by law.

1875
The German Social Democratic Party (SPD) is founded.

1886
A nationwide strike of factory workers in the US demands an 8-hour working day; the American Federation of Labor (AFL) is founded in Columbus, Ohio.

1889
The Great Dock Strike in London secures wage increases and overtime pay.

1892
French workers strike 261 times against 500 companies.

1900
The Labour Representation Committee is founded in London (renamed the Labour Party in 1906).

This painting of 1886 by German-born artist Robert Koehler (1850–1917) is called simply The Strike. Koehler based it on events he had seen in Germany, England and the USA.

Art and Literature

Artists and designers appreciated the new range of products, technology, and comforts that the Industrial Revolution provided. But they were also concerned about the quality of mass production and the living standards of working people. The machine age had changed everyone's lives. Newspaper publishers and advertisers thrived as their readership expanded. Writers had new outlets for their commentaries on society, including monthly periodicals and stage dramatizations. They all took advantage of the new opportunities.

Man reading a newspaper in London, in the late 19 century.

This silver and glass container was made in 1900 by Charles R. Ashbee (1863–1942), an English designer who founded the Guild of Handicrafts in the East End of London.

This Morris wallpaper of 1876 has typical intertwined floral motifs.

Advertising

From the mid-19th century there was an advertising boom in newspapers and magazines, as well as on hoardings and blank city walls. This helped to widen the market for new factory-produced goods. The development of mass color printing on large surfaces, by a process called chromolithography, furthered the progress of advertising posters. Leading artists took to designing and illustrating them.

Cute images, such as this one advertising soap, were popular with the public.

Arts and Crafts Movement

By the mid-19th century some artists were concerned that mass production in factories was leading to low design standards and lack of individuality. The English artist, poet, and socialist reformer William Morris (1834–96) led the Arts and Crafts movement, which stressed the artistic importance of everyday objects and the links between art and industry. Morris founded his own company in 1861 to produce furniture, carpets, and other household furnishings.

Developing technology helped the newspaper industry. Steam-powered presses such as this, invented by German printer Friedrich Koenig, were first introduced to print The Times in 1814.

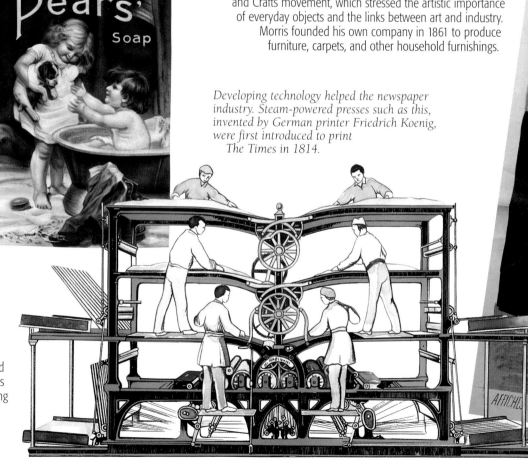

Newspapers

In Britain, The Times newspaper was first published in 1785 and the Observer six years later. Early in the following century, London had no fewer than 52 papers. The sales of national newspapers were helped when the Stamp Tax on them was abolished in 1855. In that year the Daily Telegraph was launched and sold for one penny, competing directly with the four-penny Times. The railway revolution eased distribution and brought more publications to working-class readers.

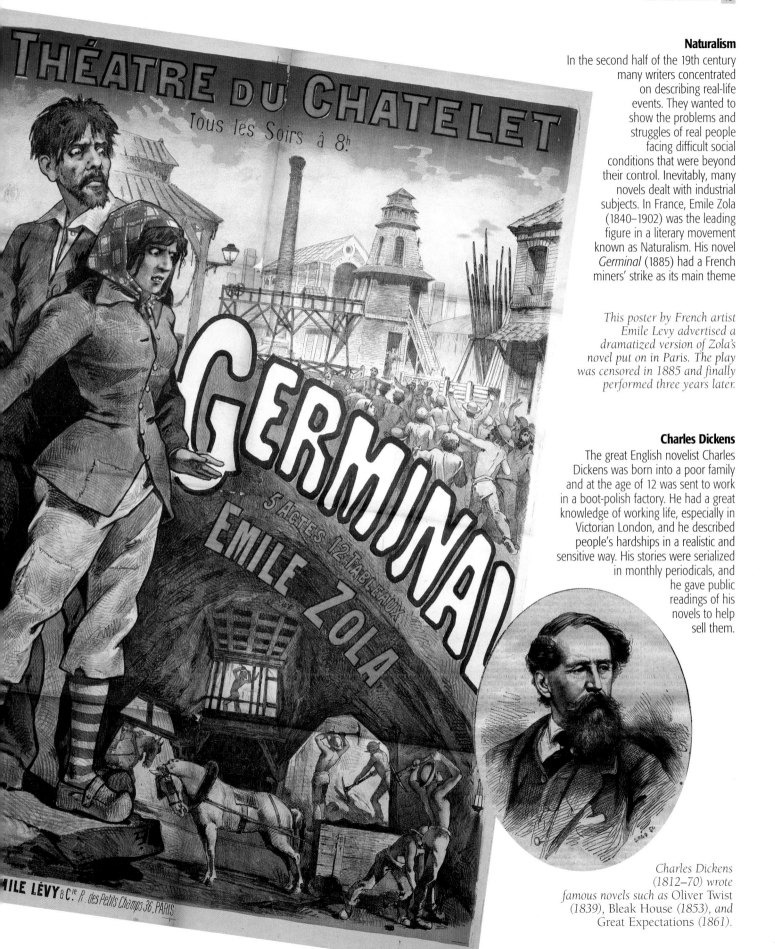

Naturalism

In the second half of the 19th century many writers concentrated on describing real-life events. They wanted to show the problems and struggles of real people facing difficult social conditions that were beyond their control. Inevitably, many novels dealt with industrial subjects. In France, Emile Zola (1840–1902) was the leading figure in a literary movement known as Naturalism. His novel *Germinal* (1885) had a French miners' strike as its main theme

This poster by French artist Émile Levy advertised a dramatized version of Zola's novel put on in Paris. The play was censored in 1885 and finally performed three years later.

Charles Dickens

The great English novelist Charles Dickens was born into a poor family and at the age of 12 was sent to work in a boot-polish factory. He had a great knowledge of working life, especially in Victorian London, and he described people's hardships in a realistic and sensitive way. His stories were serialized in monthly periodicals, and he gave public readings of his novels to help sell them.

Charles Dickens (1812–70) wrote famous novels such as Oliver Twist *(1839),* Bleak House *(1853), and* Great Expectations *(1861).*

Glossary

Anthrax An often lethal disease in humans and other animals caused by bacteria.

Bourgeoisie A term used to describe a social class of merchants, or wealthy middle class people.

Capital In economics, a term used to describe money usually used to start or maintain a business.

Cholera An infectious disease that humans catch by eating food or drinking water that is contaminated with cholera bacteria.

Collective action When people get together in a group to obtain a common goal.

Communism A political system or philosophy that seeks to establish an egalitarian (equal for all) society where there are no social classes and property is owned equally by all.

Conglomerate A large company made up of many sections all carrying out different kinds of business.

Cotton mill A factory with machinery used to spin and weave cotton into textiles (fabrics).

Crop rotation A farming practice where a series of different crops are grown in sequence on the same area of land so that it doesn't become depleted or infertile.

Customs duties A tariff or tax paid when goods are imported or exported from one country or region to another.

Enclosure A process by which commonly owned land becomes privately owned.

Entrepreneur A person who owns a company and is responsible for the risks and general outcome.

Feudalism A way of organizing a society so that everyone within it has set rights and responsibilities. It was typical of Europe in the Middle Ages, when local lords gave land in exchange for military service.

Goldsmith A craftsperson who specializes in working with gold and other precious metals, usually to make jewelry, utensils, or ceremonial objects.

Hierarchy The arrangement of people or objects into an order of ranking, such as from bottom to top or from worst to best.

Ingot A bar of metal, often gold.

Locomotive A railway vehicle that powers a train so that it can move along the rails.

Loom A machine or device used to weave thread into fabric.

Luddites A social movement of British artisans who protested against changes brought about by the Industrial Revolution, often by destroying mechanical looms.

Molten A hard substance, usually metal or rock, that has become liquid after being exposed to high temperatures.

Monotonous Repetitive or dull.

Morse code A way of encoding information into sequences of short or long sounds, pulses, or marks so that it can be sent by telegraph.

Mortgage The transfer of property to a lender (usually a bank) as security for a debt.

Peasant A farm worker who survives by working a small plot of land

Pedestrian A person moving on foot.

Periodical A publication, such as a newspaper or magazine, that appears in a new edition on a regular schedule.

Poorhouse Also known as a workhouse, where poor people were housed and had to work hard in harsh conditions to earn their keep.

Proletariat A class of society that doesn't own property or the means of production but works in exchange for wages.

Physicist A scientist who studies physics including basic concepts such as force, energy, and mass.

Rural Of the countryside.

Sanitation Ways of preventing humans from having contact with wastes, such as sewage, that can cause disease.

Sawmill A place where trees and logs are cut into boards.

Shareholders A person or company that owns shares in a joint stock company.

Smallpox An infectious human disease that killed millions of people until it was eradicated (wiped out) at the end of the 20th century.

Smelting A process of heating ores (rock) so that they release metals, such as iron.

Spinning jenny A spinning wheel with many spools invented during the Industrial Revolution that drastically reduced the amount of work needed to produce thread.

Sporadically From time to time, not on a regular basis.

Steam engine An engine that is powered by heated water vapor, or steam.

Strike Also called a strike action, where work is stopped because workers refuse to perform their jobs, usually because they want better pay or working conditions.

Telegraph A machine for transmitting and receiving messages over long distances.

Tenant farmer A farmer who works on land owned by a landlord.

Textile A flexible material or fabric made by weaving, knitting, knotting, or pressing fibers together.

Thresher A machine or device that first separates the head of a stalk of grain from the straw, and then further separates the kernel from the rest of the head.

Trade Union An organization of workers who have banded together to achieve common goals such as better wages, hours, or working conditions.

Typhus A group of diseases caused by bacteria that is carried by lice.

Urban Of the city (as opposed to the countryside).

Wage labor Where workers sell their labor (or work) to employers who pay money for it.

Index